The History of the Ocean House

by Ardith M. Schneider

Table of Contents

This book is available at the Ocean House Boutiques, The Cooked Goose, The Savoy Bookshop & Cafe in Westerly RI and Amazon.com

Looking West at Watch Hill During the Late 1800s

Pictured below is an enhanced rendition of Watch Hill by an unknown artist. The Ocean House (built in 1868) was probably only 5 or 6 years old. Although one smaller hotel, the Columbia House, has not been built, there are 3 others that are on the harbor side and obscured by the hill: the Bay View, Narraganssett and Plimpton Houses. There were very few residences, like *Catlin Cottage* at this time.

The Watch Hill, for which the village is named, is very prominent. Both the Native Americans and the colonists used this bluff as a lookout. The peninsula offered not only a strategic marine location for a lighthouse and observation point but also a spectacular view of the sunrises and sunsets, Fishers and Block Island Sounds and the Pawcatuck River.

In the 19th Century, with the advent and growth of tourism, people wanted to escape the congestion and noise of manufacturing cities. Most visitors to Watch Hill came from the north and west, traveling by rail to Stonington and then by steamer to the village. Just as it is today, Watch Hill was a summer destination back in the 1800s.

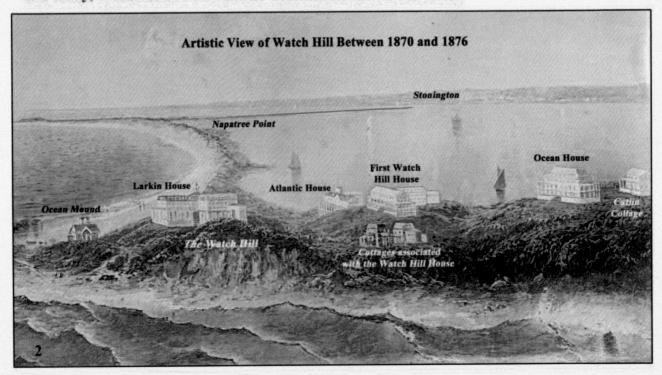

Artistic View of Watch Hill Between 1870 and 1876

1868

The First Ocean House

The Ocean House was built in 1868 for George Nash, whose father was Jonathan Nash, the first Watch Hill lighthouse keeper. Jonathan Nash was the lighthouse keeper from 1808 to 1833, and he was also the first person to take on seasonal boarders in Watch Hill. What an idea!

A Mansard roof wing was added to the north, as was a tower with a tall hip roof (circa 1900). The tower was added to accomodate the elevator. In 1903, because of the growing popularity of the hotel, two massive east wings were added facing the beach. This greatly expanded the number of rooms, and the dining room could now seat up to 500. At its peak the hotel had over 154 rooms for guests.

Views from the Late 1800s

An early photo of Bluff Avenue (circa 1892) looking north. Identifiable buildings (left to right) are the corner of the New Watch Hill House, the original Watch Hill House in front of the Ocean House and a white cottage, *The Dunes*. Right foreground shows the Alsop and Grant cottages and the Watch Hill House bowling alley sticking out of the back.

This photo, of the southwest side of Bluff Avenue, shows (left to right) the chapel, the original Watch Hill House with three chimneys, the Ocean House and the Bowling Alley (foreground).

The Ocean House and Environs - Photo taken from Sunset Hill

Hotel guests would stroll to the gazebo on Sunset Hill to watch the sunset.

Photo on the left is Sunset Hill before the villa also called *Sunset Hill* was built. Below are the gazebo and *Sunset Hill* under construction.

Both of these hotel scenes, photographed from slightly different angles, were taken before the Watch Hill Chapel was built in 1876.

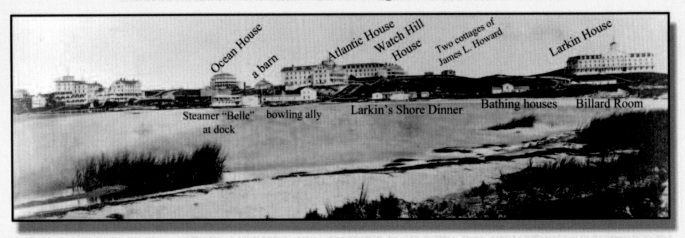

Hotels grouped at the left (above): The James Nash House, The Joseph Nash House, Plimpton House (with cupola), Bay View House, and Narragansett House.

A very stark hotel scene, circa 1870, showing from left to right: Ocean House, Plimpton House, Bay View (annex of Plimpton House), Narragansett House, Atlantic House and the Watch Hill House.

"Watch Hill has hotels, but not a single tree. To pacify guests, landscape scenes are hung in the parlors of the hotels." *Stonington Mirror* 6/28/1877

The Ocean House is barely visible in this photo (circa 1882) with the chapel spire to the left of the dome. The Columbia House had not been built (1890). The Howard Cottage (1879), seen to the right of the Watch Hill House, was the first seasonal residence in Watch Hill.

A view of East Beach from the Atlantic side of the peninsula, early 1900. The Ocean House is in the center foreground and the Watch Hill House, in the distance.

Hotel Map - Early 1900s

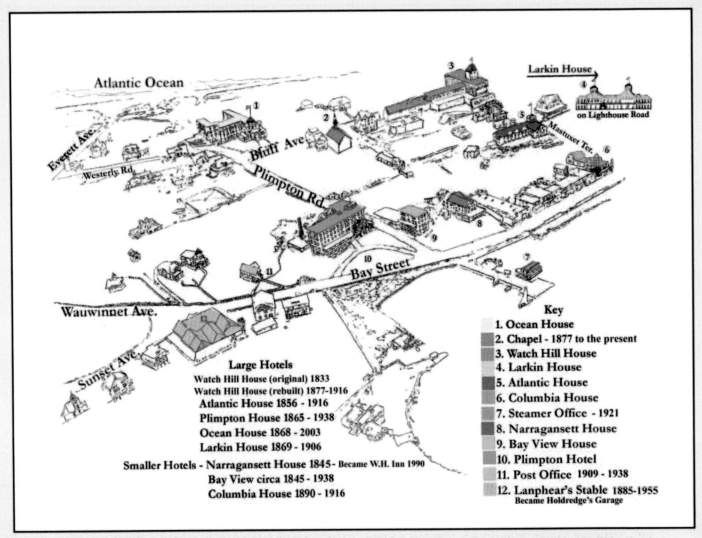

Key
1. Ocean House
2. Chapel - 1877 to the present
3. Watch Hill House
4. Larkin House
5. Atlantic House
6. Columbia House
7. Steamer Office - 1921
8. Narragansett House
9. Bay View House
10. Plimpton Hotel
11. Post Office 1909 - 1938
12. Lanphear's Stable 1885-1955
Became Holdredge's Garage

Large Hotels
Watch Hill House (original) 1833
Watch Hill House (rebuilt) 1877-1916
Atlantic House 1856 - 1916
Plimpton House 1865 - 1938
Ocean House 1868 - 2003
Larkin House 1869 - 1906

Smaller Hotels - Narragansett House 1845- Became W.H. Inn 1990
Bay View circa 1845 - 1938
Columbia House 1890 - 1916

"Each hotel has its own orchestra; and hops. Whist parties, ping pong, promenading and flirting, are some of the evening amusements." *A Brief History of Watch Hill* by Annie Burdick

Here is a slightly different view (circa 1912), from the map on page 8, taken from an early seaplane. Pawcatuck Avenue is in the foreground. Photo below, taken from Lighthouse Point, shows the Watch Hill House and the Ocean House (circa 1915). Note the smaller dome on the Ocean House.

89-79

A Look at the Village

Electricity had come to the village by 1895. In the postcard above people are waiting for the trolley at the south end of Bay Street right in front of the merry-go-round. The picture below shows Bay Street looking north. The dome of the Columbia House stands out in both postcards (where the Olympia Tea Room is today).

Pictured above is the trolley terminal at the end of Bay Street. The sign on the restaurant next to the theatre says, "Regular Dinner 50 cents." The scene below looks up at the side of the Watch Hill House with the Atlantic House on the left and the Columbia House in front of it.

Arrival in Watch Hill

Of great importance to the Watch Hill visitor were the steamers and the docks. From the mid 1800s to the early 1900s Watch Hill was virtually an island only approachable by water. Above is the main dock on Bay Street with the popular Larkin Shore Dinners to the right and the Larkin House behind it. Below is the Block Island ferry stopping in Watch Hill from New London. The lighthouse is in the background.

Many hotel guests took day trips to Block Island.

The steamer *Watch Hill* (above) had scheduled trips between Stonington and Watch Hill - twenty-five cents, round trip. The steamer operated from 1899 to 1920 with connections to New London and Norwich.

SUNDAY, JUNE 26th
—THE—
--STEAMER ELLA--
Will make an excursion to
WATCH HILL
and return. Leaving Norwich at 9 a. m.
FARE 50 Cents.
Clam Bake and Shore Dinner at the Hill.
Je25f8

"The cost was only 50 cents to travel to Watch Hill aboard the Steamer Ella from Norwich." (Norwich Bulletin, June 25, 1897).

Travel on Land

Watch Hill was reached mainly by steamer until 1894 when a railway company started a trolley between Westerly and Watch Hill; here passengers disembark.

A very lively downtown trolley scene circa 1910. In the upper left corner is the Columbia House where the Olympia Tea Room is today.

The guests rode bikes and drove motor cars.

Bicyling was a popular hotel activity. Above cyclists pedal toward the Ocean House on Westerly Road, circa 1898. The front biker is almost at the intersection of Everett Avenue. Below automobiles wait for bathers across from the merry-go-round on Larkin Road about 15 years later.

What the Guests Viewed from the Ocean House Windows

From the front window looking southwest.

Left to right: The Watch Hill House, two annexes (Mastuxet Lodge and Ninigret Lodge), the chapel and Collins Cottage.

Looking up Westerly Road from the northeast side of the Ocean House. Note the little schoolhouse in the foreground and the tiny outhouse, circled in red, behind it.

The Schoolhouse - A History of Its Own

The Watch Hill Schoolhouse was built
in 1852. It was a very simple building
that could hold up to 19 pupils. That
capacity was reached before the school
was closed in 1901. By then the trolley
had come to Watch Hill, so the children
could go to the school in Avondale.

About a decade later the schoolhouse
became a gift shop which two Stevenson
sisters ran for about 28 years.
That venture ended with the hurricane
of '38 which took the sisters out to sea
from their house on Fort Road.
The cottage is now rented to Ocean
House guests and used as an *Artist's
Cottage.*

Hotel Activities

July 11 -1931

Dear K. This is where we sit in stormy weather and we have had plenty of that. Last night over forty airmen were here & this a.m. we watched their planes fly off - It is lovely today, but the beach is quite a walk from the hotel so I sit on the porch

most of the time. Home Monday.

Games, Parties and Festivals

Baseball games were organized by the staffs of the various hotels. The baseball diamond was located behind the Ocean House.

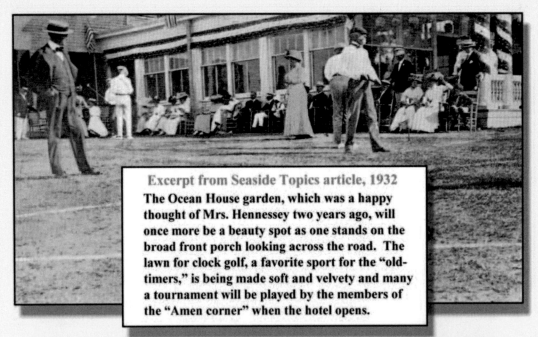

The Ocean House Garden
Watch Hill, Rhode Island

Gardens across from the Ocean House during the 1930s. This postcard looks south at *Collins Cottage* next to the chapel.

The flower garden is still in place across Bluff Avenue from the hotel in this photo from the 1940s. There was a walkway down to the cocktail lounge beyond the rotunda on the south porch.

Caption from an Ocean House brochure: *In our comfortable Cocktail Lounge there is music nightly and during the cocktail hour. Our Friday and Saturday night dances are special events with an excellent orchestra.* **21**

Porch and Interior Postcards of the Ocean House

Ocean House, Entrance
Watch Hill, Rhode Island

Sun Porch faces the southwest with the rotunda columns in the middle.

Postcard of the dining room is circa 1960.

The aerial view above shows the large white *Harkness House* (built in 1930) in the fore-ground and the grey *Dormitory* (behind the Ocean House) where the staff lived during the season. Photo below (circa 1960) shows the configuration of the back oceanside wings and a golf chipping green off the side porch.

Pictures taken from an Ocean House brochure, circa 1960.

Buffet and beverage service is available on the
Marine Deck, overlooking sea and rolling dunes.

Map from the back of the brochure.

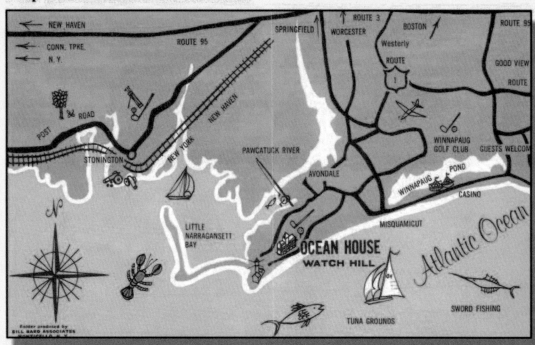

The Ocean House Closes - 2003

Photomontage by
Ardi Schneider '03

 After the Ocean House closed its doors at the end of the 2003 season, the community
wondered what would happen to the yellow icon. Fire codes in Rhode Island had been
upgraded preventing occupancy of the hotel. There were many proposals and much
controversy about the 13-acre oceanfront property. Would the hotel go out in the sunset
as the image above might suggest? Would it be torn down and replaced by McMansions?
Would it (could it) be reconstructed?

Preservationists banded together, but studies indicated that the basic structure of the
building could not conform to modern building codes. In 2004 Centerbrook Architects,
hired by WatchHill resident Chuck Royce, devised a plan for replication of the hotel.
It is a new structure; but in the larger context of preservation, its essence is preserved.

Replication

Architectural elements were harvested out of the Ocean House. Some were saved and stored; and others, like the windows, were carefully replicated.

A patriotic swag is seen waving in the breeze as the Ocean House closes down.

The office trailer is seen through the newly installed front Palladian window.

Old and new railings and balusters standing side by side. Photo taken 2009.

Fanlight doorway in storage

27

Arrow (in photo above) shows where the
original elevator was located. Photo in
upper right shows the elevator in storage.
It is now expanded, with some replicated
parts, and installed in the main lobby area.
Photo below is from the inside of the
elevator looking up.

Many art deco chandeliers, like the one
shown in the main hall of the old hotel
photo, have been refurbished and they
are hanging from the ceiling of the
Drawing Room on the ground floor of
the hotel.

Fireplace Mantel

Original fireplace

Stones carefully sorted in buckets and stored.

Being rebuilt 2009

Mantel decorated for the holidays.   29

Demolition

On a cold rainy day at the end of December 2005, the demolition began on the venerable old hotel. It was painted white first, to encapsulate the lead in the yellow paint. Television crews and reporters attended.

The preparation work of leveling the ground, removing large rocks and putting in a new septic system was the task for 2007. The beginning of the foundation was started in the spring of 2008.

Construction Phase

"The New Ocean House" A Complete
Description of the Project, May 2006

"Topping-Off" Ceremony, July 11, 2008
The tree on top symbolizes "Good Luck."

Ribbon Cutting Ceremony - May 2010.

North Wing - Westerly Road

Extensive scaffolding
surrounded the building
in this photograph. It took
four years to build this
magnificent new structure.

This pictorial story follows a small oceanside boarding house to its evolution as an iconic Victorian hotel.

In May of 2006, Bluff Avenue LLC made the commitment to replicate the Ocean House as it was in its heyday, 1908.

Today's Ocean House

From a distance the dome of the Ocean House, with its distinctive circular windows, looks the same in this photo (2010) as in the late 1800s when it was constructed. The metamorphosis from a small three story summer boarding house in 1868, through many additions to an elegant Forbes five-star resort has been a collaborative effort using great talent and resources. Even as the hotel, in later years, fell short of its heyday reputation up to the 1930s, it was still an icon and a landmark. Now, in its replicated glory with outstanding architectural detail and modern amenities, its year-round presence is more than an asset to the community. 33

The Ocean House celebrates patriotism and the holidays!

photo thanks to L. Nigrelli

A gingerbread Ocean House.

Colorful candy jars are always full.

35

Acknowledgements

Material for this book was excerpted from: *Watch Hill Then & Now,* by Roberta Burkhardt, Michael Beddard and Ardith Schneider, 2005; *A Penny for Your Thoughts,* by Marian Burke, Roberta Burkhardt and Ardith Schneider, 2009; A Brief History of Watch Hill by Annie Burdick, 1903 and *Watch Hill Historic District,* Prepared by Rupert O. Jones, Jr., R.I. Historical Preservation Commission, 1988. Also used for reference were *Watch Hill Through Time* by Chaplin Bradford Barnes, 2005 and *Watch Hill: By River and By Sea* by Brigid Rooney Smith, 2004. The idea for the book came from Annie Rehlander, Ocean House Boutique. Additional information and material was provided by former Ocean House Operations Manager, Michael Brankert. Many thanks to editors: Helen Jankoski, Liz Sayre and Nelson White.

"The Watch Hill community of today, while altered by Mother Nature, human nature and technology, still retains many of the architectural flavors of the late 19th and early 20th centuries and the integrity of its historic character." Joanna Burkhardt, *Watch Hill Then and Now.*

Newly replicated dome with the "Ocean House" being attached.

Made in the USA
Middletown, DE
07 December 2017